D1235695

THE KOREAN VERBS GUIDE
Vol. 2

written and designed by
TalkToMeInKorean

1판 1쇄	1st edition published	2013. 12. 2
1판 8쇄	8th edition published	2019. 3. 12
지은이	Written by	TalkToMeInKorean
책임편집	Edited by	안효진 Hyojin Ahn, 스테파니 베이츠 Stephanie Bates
디자인	Design by	선윤아 Yoona Sun
일러스트	Illustration by	장성원 Sungwon Jang
사진	Photograph by	라이언 카발 Ryan Cabal
녹음	Voice Recording by	안효진 Hyojin Ahn
펴낸곳	Published by	롱테일북스 Longtail Books
펴낸이	Publisher	이수영 Su Young Lee
편집	Copy-edited by	김보경 Florence Kim
주소	Address	04043 서울 마포구 양화로 12길 16-9(서교동) 북앤빌딩 3층 롱테일북스
		3rd Floor, Book-And Bldg. 16-9, Yanghwa-ro 12-gil, Mapo-gu, Seoul, KOREA
이메일	E-mail	TTMIK@longtailbooks.co.kr
ISBN	978-89-5605-706-4	13710

THE KOREAN VERBS GUIDE

Vol.2

한국어 학습자가 반드시 알아야 할
동사 가이드

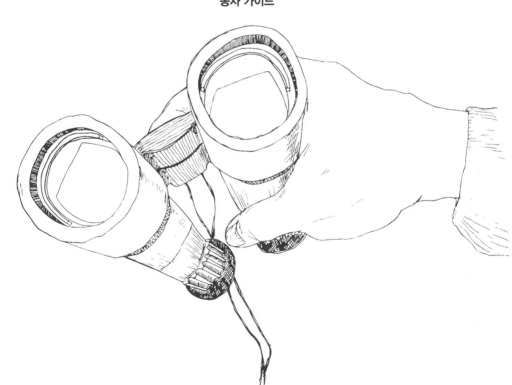

Index for Volume 1

Index for Volume 2

vol. 2

만나다
to meet (up)

The Korean Verbs Guide - vol.2

Conjugation

man-na-da

Present	Past	Future / Guessing	Present Progressive
만나요	만났어요	만날 거예요	만나고 있어요
mannayo	mannasseoyo	mannal geoyeyo	mannago isseoyo

Imperative

만나세요	만나요	만나	만나라
mannaseyo	mannayo	manna	mannara

Modifier

만난	만나는	만날	만나던	만났던
mannan	mannaneun	mannal	mannadeon	mannattteon

Want	Can
만나고 싶어요	만날 수 있어요
mannago sipeoyo	mannal su isseoyo

Don't (Imperative)	Whether or not		
만나지 마세요	만나는지	만났는지	만날지
mannaji maseyo	mannaneunji	mannanneunji	mannaljji

(tell someone) that	(tell someone) to
만난다고	만나라고
mannandago	manarago

9

Sample Sentences

1. 내일 석진 씨 만날 거예요.
   I'm going to meet Seokjin tomorrow.

2. 아직 몇 시에 만날지 안 정했어요.
   We haven't decided what time we are going to meet yet.

3. 다음주에 누구 만난다고 했죠?
   Who did you say you were going to meet next week?

4. 지금 친구 만나고 있어요.
   I am with my friends right now.

5. 우리 언제 처음 만났는지 기억해요?
   Do you remember when we first met?

Quiz

1. 다음주에 홍대에서 민정 씨 (   ).
   I'm going to meet Minjeong next week in Hongdae.

2. 파리에서 클라라 씨 언제 (   ) 했죠?
   When did you say you were going to meet Clara in Paris?

3. 우리 내일 언제 (   ) 정해요.
   Let's decide when we will meet tomorrow.

Answers :
1. 만날 거예요 / 2. 만난다고 / 3. 만날지

얻다

to get, to acquire, to gain

Conjugation

Present	Past	Future / Guessing	Present Progressive
얻어요	얻었어요	얻을 거예요	얻고 있어요
eodeoyo	eodeosseoyo	eodeul geoyeyo	eotgo isseoyo

Imperative

얻으세요	얻어요	얻어	얻어라
eodeuseyo	eodeoyo	eodeo	eodeora

Modifier

얻은	얻는	얻을	얻던	얻었던
eodeun	eonneun	eodeul	eottteon	eodeotteon

Want

얻고 싶어요
eotkko sipeoyo

Can

얻을 수 있어요
eodeul su isseoyo

Don't (Imperative)

얻지 마세요
eotjji maseyo

Whether or not

얻는지	얻었는지	얻을지
eonneunji	eodeonneunji	eodeuljji

(tell someone) that

얻는다고
eonneundago

(tell someone) to

얻으라고
eodeurago

Sample Sentences

1. 지난번 일을 계기로 자신감을 많이 얻었어요.
   I gained a lot of confidence after finishing the last task.

2. 제가 인터넷에서 얻은 정보가 잘못된 정보인가 봐요.
   It seems that the information I got from the Internet was wrong.

3. 방 세 개짜리 집을 얻고 싶어요.
   I want to get a house with three rooms.

4. 여기서 많은 정보를 얻을 수 있어요.
   You can find a lot of information here.

5. 그 회사 홈페이지에 가면 많은 정보를 얻을 수 있어요.
   If you go to that company's homepage, you can find a lot of information.

Quiz

1. 어제 있었던 일로 자신감을 조금 (   ).
   I gained a little bit of confidence after what happened yesterday.

2. 어제 지영 씨한테 (   ) 정보가 잘못된 정보였어요.
   The information I got from Jiyoung yesterday was wrong.

3. 거기서도 여행에 관련된 정보를 (   )?
   Can you find information about traveling there too?

Answers :
1. 얻었어요 / 2. 얻은 / 3. 얻을 수 있어요

13

혼자서도 10분 안에
만들 수 있어요.

I can even make it by myself in ten minutes.

만들다
to make

Conjugation

만들다

man-deul-da

Present	Past	Future / Guessing	Present Progressive
만들어요	만들었어요	만들 거예요	만들고 있어요
mandeureoyo	mandeureosseoyo	mandeul geoyeyo	mandeulgo isseoyo

Imperative

만드세요	만들어요	만들어	만들어라
mandeuseyo	mandeureoyo	mandeureo	mandeureora

Modifier

만든	만드는	만들	만들던	만들었던
mandeun	mandeuneun	mandeul	mandeuldeon	mandeureottteon

Want

만들고 싶어요

mandeulgo sipeoyo

Can

만들 수 있어요

mandeul su isseoyo

Don't (Imperative)

만들지 마세요

mandeulji maseyo

Whether or not

만드는지	만들었는지	만들지
mandeuneunji	mandeureonneunji	mandeuljji

(tell someone) that

만든다고

mandeundago

(tell someone) to

만들라고

mandeullago

The Korean Verbs Guide - vol.2

Sample Sentences

Track
53

1. 이거 친구 주려고 만들었어요.
   I made this to give to my friend.

2. 제가 만든 떡볶이가 맛이 없어요?
   Was the tteokbokki I made not delicious?

3. 재밌는 영상을 만들고 싶어요.
   I want to make funny videos.

4. 어떻게 만드는지 모르겠어요.
   I don't know how to make it.

5. 혼자서도 10분 안에 만들 수 있어요.
   I can even make it by myself in ten minutes.

Quiz

1. 제 친구가 (   ) 김밥 맛있어요?
   Did the Gimbap my friend made taste delicious?

2. 좋은 노래를 (   ).
   I want to make good songs.

3. 어디서 (   ) 아세요?
   Do you know where they make it?

잃어버리다
to lose (something)

Conjugation

Present	Past	Future / Guessing	Present Progressive
잃어버려요	잃어버렸어요	잃어버릴 거예요	—
ireobeoryeoyo	ireobeoryeosseoyo	irreobeoril geoyeyo	

Imperative

—	—	—	—

Modifier

잃어버린	잃어버리는	잃어버릴	잃어버리던	잃어버렸던
ireobeorin	ireobeorineun	ireobeoril	ireobeorideon	ireobeoryeotteon

Want	*Can*
—	잃어버릴 수 있어요
	ireobeoril su isseoyo

Don't (Imperative)	*Whether or not*		
잃어버리지 마세요	잃어버리는지	잃어버렸는지	잃어버릴지
ireobeoriji maseyo	ireobeorineunji	ireobeoryeonneunji	ireobeoriljji

(tell someone) that	*(tell someone) to*
잃어버린다고	—
ireobeorindago	

19

Sample Sentences

1. 저는 물건을 잘 잃어버려요.
   I lose things often.

2. 중요한 거니까 잃어버리지 마세요.
   This is really important, so don't lose it.

3. 어디서 잃어버렸는지 알아요?
   Do you know where you lost it?

4. 잃어버린 장갑 찾았어요?
   Did you find the gloves you lost?

5. 작년에 잃어버렸던 책을 침대 밑에서 찾았어요.
   I found the book that I lost last year under my bed.

Quiz

1. 저는 평소에 물건 잘 안 (   ).
   I don't usually lose things.

2. 비싼거니까 절대로 (   ).
   It's expensive, so don't ever lose it, please.

3. 언제 (   ) 기억나요?
   Do you remember when you lost it?

 Answers :
1. 잃어버려요 / 2. 잃어버리지 마세요 / 3. 잃어버렸는지

잊어버리다
to forget

Conjugation

Present	Past	Future / Guessing	Present Progressive
잊어버려요	잊어버렸어요	잊어버릴 거예요	—
ijeobeoryeoyo	ijeobeoryeosseoyo	ijeobeoril geoyeyo	

Imperative

잊어버리세요	잊어버려요	잊어버려	잊어버려라
ijeobeoriseyo	ijeobeoryeoyo	ijeobeoryeo	ijeobeoryeora

Modifier

잊어버린	잊어버리는	잊어버릴	잊어버리던	잊어버렸던
ijeobeorin	ijeobeorineun	ijeobeoril	ijeobeorideon	ijeobeoryeottteon

Want

잊어버리고 싶어요
ijeobeorigo sipeoyo

Can

잊어버릴 수 있어요
ijeobeoril su isseoyo

Don't (Imperative)

잊어버리지 마세요
ijeobeoriji maseyo

Whether or not

잊어버리는지	잊어버렸는지	잊어버릴지
ijeobeorineunji	ijeobeoryeonneunji	ijeobeoriljji

(tell someone) that

잊어버린다고
ijeobeorindago

(tell someone) to

잊어버리라고
ijeobeorirago

The Korean Verbs Guide - vol.2

Sample Sentences

1. 수영 씨 결혼식이 언제인지 잊어버렸어요.
   I forgot when Sooyoung's wedding is.

2. 그냥 잊어버리세요.
   Just forget it.

3. 어차피 시험 끝나면 오늘 외운 거 다 잊어버릴 거예요.
   Regardless, I am going to forget all of the things I memorized today once
   the exam is over.

4. 저는 사람들 이름을 자꾸 잊어버려요.
   I forget people's names a lot.

5. 친구가 지갑을 잃어버려서 속상해하길래 그냥 잊어버리라고 했어요.
   My friend was upset because he lost his wallet, so I just told him to forget
   about it.

Quiz

1. 재석 씨 연주회가 몇 시인지 (   ).
   I forgot what time Jaeseok's recital is.

2. 제 친구는 중요한 일은 다 (   ).
   A friend of mine forgets all important things.

3. 친구가 좋아하는 여자한테 고백했다가 거절당해서 슬퍼하길래 그냥
   (   ) 했어요.
   My friend was upset because he was rejected by the girl he likes when he
   confessed to her, so I just told him to forget about her.

Answers :
1. 잊어버렸어요 / 2. 잊어버려요 / 3. 잊어버리라고

23

좋다

to be good;
to like

The Korean Verbs Guide - vol.2

Conjugation

좋다
jo-ta

Present	Past	Future / Guessing	Present Progressive
좋아요	좋았어요	좋을 거예요	—
joayo	joasseoyo	joeul geoyeyo	

Imperative

— — — —

Modifier

좋은	—	좋을	좋던	좋았던
joeun		jo-eul	joteon	joattteon

Want	Can
—	좋을 수 있어요
	jo-eul su isseoyo

Don't (Imperative)	Whether or not
—	좋은지 좋았는지 좋을지
	jo-eunji joanneunji joeuljji

(tell someone) that	(tell someone) to
좋다고	—
jotago	

Sample Sentences

1. 뭐가 좋은지 저도 모르겠어요.
   I don't know which one is good, either.

2. 지나고 나니까 좋았던 기억밖에 없어요.
   Now that it's over, I only have good memories left.

3. 언제가 좋을지 말해 주세요.
   Let me know when would be a good time for you.

4. 선생님이 좋다고 하셨어요.
   My teacher said it was good.

5. 사람이 많으면 많을수록 좋아요.
   The more people, the better.

Quiz

1. 지금 생각해보면 (   ) 기억이 나빴던 기억보다 더 많아요.
   Now that I look back, I have more good memories left than bad memories.

2. 누가 이 역할을 맡으면 (   ) 추천해 주세요.
   Please recommend (someone) who would be good to take on this role.

3. 패스트푸드는 적게 먹으면 먹을수록 (   ).
   The less junk food you eat, the better.

Answers :
1. 좋았던 / 2. 좋을지 / 3. 좋아요.

좋아하다

to like

Conjugation

좋아하다
jo·a·ha·da

Present	Past	Future / Guessing	Present Progressive
좋아해요	좋아했어요	좋아할 거예요	좋아하고 있어요
joahaeyo	joahaesseoyo	joahal geoyeyo	joahago isseoyo

Imperative

—   —   —   —

Modifier

좋아한	좋아하는	좋아할	좋아하던	좋아했던
joahan	joahaneun	joahal	joahadeon	joahaettteon

Want	Can
좋아하고 싶어요	좋아할 수 있어요
joahago sipeoyo	joahal su isseoyo

Don't (Imperative)	Whether or not		
좋아하지 마세요	좋아하는지	좋아했는지	좋아할지
joahaji maseyo	joahaneunji	joahaenneunji	joahaljji

(tell someone) that	(tell someone) to
좋아한다고	좋아하라고
joahandago	joaharago

The Korean Verbs Guide - vol.2

Sample Sentences

1. 제가 뭘 좋아하는지 아직도 몰라요?
   You still don't know what I like?

2. 제일 좋아하는 운동이 뭐예요?
   What is your favorite sport?

3. 와인 좋아해요?
   Do you like wine?

4. 공짜 너무 좋아하지 마세요.
   Don't like free things too much.

5. 이 선물을 받으면 친구가 정말 좋아할 거예요.
   My friend would really like it if she got this as a present.

Quiz

1. 경화 씨가 꽃 (   ) 몰랐어요.
   I didn't know Kyung-hwa likes flowers.

2. 요즘 제일 (   ) 드라마가 뭐예요?
   What drama do you like the best these days?

3. 강아지 (   )?
   Do you like puppies?

29

이 분이 마시는 커피랑 똑같은 걸로
주세요.

Please give me the same coffee this person is drinking.

마시다

to drink

Conjugation

마시다
ma-si-da

Present	Past	Future / Guessing	Present Progressive
마셔요	마셨어요	마실 거예요	마시고 있어요
masyeoyo	masyeosseoyo	masil geoyeyo	masigo isseoyo

Imperative

드세요	마셔요	마셔	마셔라
deuseyo	masyeoyo	masyeo	masyeora

Modifier

마신	마시는	마실	마시던	마셨던
masin	masineun	masil	masideon	masyeottteon

Want

마시고 싶어요
masigo sipeoyo

Can

마실 수 있어요
masil su isseyo

Don't (Imperative)

마시지 마세요
masiji maseyo

Whether or not

마시는지	마셨는지	마실지
masineunji	masyeonneunji	masiljji

(tell someone) that

마신다고
masindago

(tell someone) to

마시라고
masirago

The Korean Verbs Guide - vol.2

Sample Sentences

1. 이 분이 마시는 커피랑 똑같은 걸로 주세요.
   Please give me the same coffee this person is drinking.

2. 물 마시고 싶어요.
   I want to drink water.

3. 커피 누구랑 마셨어요?
   With whom did you drink coffee?

4. 이 물은 더러우니까 마시지 마세요.
   This water is dirty, so please don't drink it.

5. 우유를 따뜻하게 데워서 마실 거예요.
   I will drink the milk after heating it up.

Quiz

1. 저 사람이 (   ) 주스랑 똑같은 걸로 주세요.
   Please give me the same juice that person is drinking.

2. 스무디 (   ).
   I want to drink a smoothie.

3. 이 음료수 (   ). 맛이 이상해요.
   Please don't drink this beverage. It tastes weird.

정하다
to decide

Conjugation

Present	Past	Future / Guessing	Present Progressive
정해요	정했어요	정할 거예요	정하고 있어요
jeong-haeyo	jeong-haesseoyo	jeong-hal geoyeyo	jeong-hago isseoyo

Imperative

정하세요	정해요	정해	정해라
jeong-haseyo	jeong-haeyo	jeong-hae	jeong-haera

Modifier

정한	정하는	정할	정하던	정했던
jeong-han	jeong-haneun	jeong-hal	jeong-hadeon	jeong-haettteon

Want

정하고 싶어요
jeong-hago sipeopyo

Can

정할 수 있어요
jeong-hal su isseoyo

Don't (Imperative)

정하지 마세요
jeong-haji maseyo

Whether or not

정하는지	정했는지	정할지
jeong-haneunji	jeong-haenneunji	jeong-haljji

(tell someone) that

정한다고
jeong-handago

(tell someone) to

정하라고
jeong-harago

Sample Sentences

1. 저녁 뭐 먹을지 정했어요?
   Did you decide what you are going to eat for dinner?

2. 혼자서 정하지 마세요.
   Don't decide by yourself.

3. 장소랑 시간은 스테파니 씨가 정한다고 했어요.
   Stephanie will decide the time and date.

4. 지금 당장 정하라고 하면 전 어떡해요?
   If you tell me to decide right away, what am I supposed to do?

5. 이렇게 정한 이유가 있어요?
   Is there a reason why you decided (to do it) like this?

Quiz

1. 이따가 뭐 할지 (   )?
   Did you decide what you are going to do later today?

2. 지금은 아무것도 (   ).
   Don't decide anything for now, please.

3. 이 많은 걸 저 혼자 (   ) 하면 전 어떡해요?
   If you tell me to decide this many things, what am I supposed to do?

Answers :
1. 정했어요 / 2. 정하지 마세요 / 3. 정하라고

The Korean Verbs Guide - vol.2

바꾸다
to change

Condagation

Present	Past	Future / Guessing	Present Progressive
바꿔요	바꿨어요	바꿀 거예요	바꾸고 있어요
bakkwoyo	bakkwosseoyo	bakkul geoyeyo	bakkugo isseoyo

Imperative

바꾸세요	바꿔요	바꿔	바꿔라
bakkuseyo	bakkwoyo	bakkwo	bakkwora

Modifier

바꾼	바꾸는	바꿀	바꾸던	바꿨던
bakkun	bakkuneun	bakkul	bakkudeon	bakkwottteon

Want	Can
바꾸고 싶어요	바꿀 수 있어요
bakkugo sipeoyo	bakkul su isseoyo

Don't (Imperative)	Whether or not		
바꾸지 마세요	바꾸는지	바꿨는지	바꿀지
bakkuji maseyo	bakkuneunji	bakkwonneunji	bakkuljji

(tell someone) that	(tell someone) to
바꾼다고	바꾸라고
bakkundago	bakkurago

Sample Sentences

Track
60

1. 저 이름 바꿀 거예요.
   I am going to change my name.

2. 보고서 주제를 어제 바꿨어요.
   I changed the topic for my report yesterday.

3. 전화번호를 바꿨는지 몰랐어요.
   I didn't know you changed your phone number.

4. 지금 당장 일정을 바꾸라고 하세요.
   Please tell them to change the schedule immediately.

5. 핸드폰을 최신 모델로 바꾸고 싶어요.
   I want to change my phone to the newest model, too.

Quiz

1. 수미 씨 이름 (   ) 알았어요?
   You knew Soomi changed her name?

2. 전화로 계획을 (   ) 하세요.
   Please tell them to change the plan via phone.

3. 컴퓨터를 새 걸로 (   ) 싶어요.
   I want to change my computer to a new one.

Answers :
1. 바꿨는지 / 2. 바꾸라고 / 3. 바꾸고

39

알다
to know

Conjugation

Present	Past	Future / Guessing	Present Progressive
알아요	알았어요	알 거예요	알고 있어요
arayo	arasseoyo	al geoyeyo	algo isseoyo

Imperative

—	—	—	—

Modifier

안	아는	알	알던	알았던
an	aneun	al	aldeon	arattteon

Want	Can
알고 싶어요	알 수 있어요
algo sipeoyo	al su isseoyo

Don't (Imperative)	Whether or not		
—	아는지	알았는지	알지
	aneunji	aranneunji	aljji

(tell someone) that	(tell someone) to
안다고	알라고
andago	allago

Sample Sentences

Track
61

1. 이 문제의 정답을 아는 사람이 아무도 없어요?
   Is there no one who knows the answer to this question?

2. 제가 아는 사람하고 닮았어요.
   You look like someone I know.

3. 이 책을 보면 알 수 있어요.
   You will know if you look at this book.

4. 뭘 그렇게 알고 싶어요?
   What do you want to know so badly?

5. 준영 씨가 아는지 모르는지 모르겠어요.
   I don't know if Jun-yeong knows or not.

Quiz

1. 제가 한 질문의 정답을 (   ) 사람은 손 드세요.
   Anyone who knows the answer to the question I asked, please raise your hand.

2. 선생님께 여쭤보면 (   ).
   If you ask your teacher, you will find out.

3. 수아 씨가 (   ) 모르는지 물어보세요.
   Please ask if Su-ah knows or not.

Answers :
1. 아는 / 2. 알 수 있어요 / 3. 아는지

The Korean Verbs Guide - vol.2

버스 안이 정말 좁아요.

The inside of the bus is really narrow.

좁다
to be narrow,
to be small (space)

Conjugation

좁다
jopda

Present	Past	Future / Guessing	Present Progressive
좁아요	좁았어요	좁을 거예요	—
jobayo	jobasseoyo	jobeul geoyeyo	

Imperative

— — — —

Modifier

좁은	—	좁을	좁던	좁았던
jobeun		jobeul	joptteon	jobattteon

Want

—

Can

좁을 수 있어요
jobeul su isseoyo

Don't (Imperative)

—

Whether or not

좁은지	좁았는지	좁을지
jobeunji	jobanneunji	jobeuljji

(tell someone) that

좁다고
jopttago

(tell someone) to

좁으라고
jobeurago

Sample Sentences

1. 이렇게 좁은 방에 사람이 15명이나 들어올 수 있다고요?
   Are you saying that 15 people can come in a small room like this?

2. 얼마나 좁은지 물어봐 주세요.
   Please ask how small it is.

3. 열 명이 들어가면 좁을 거예요.
   If ten people go in, it will be small.

4. 저는 넓은 집보다 좁은 집이 좋아요.
   I like small houses more than wide houses.

5. 세상 참 좁아요.
   The world is really small. (What a small world.)

Quiz

1. 그렇게 (   ) 소파 위에서 잠을 자겠다고요?
   Are you saying that you are going to sleep on a small couch like that?

2. 얼마나 (   ) 눈으로 직접 확인해 주세요.
   Please check with your own eyes how small it is.

3. 거기 다섯 명이 다 앉으면 (   ).
   If all five people sit on there, it will be small.

Answers :
1. 좁은 / 2. 좁은지 / 3. 좁을 거예요

넓다

to be wide,
to be big (space)

Conjugation

Present	Past	Future / Guessing	Present Progressive
넓어요	넓었어요	넓을 거예요	—
neolbeoyo	neolbeosseoyo	neolbeul geoyeyo	

Imperative

—	—	—	—

Modifier

넓은	—	넓을	넓던	넓었던
neolbeun		neolbeul	neoltteon	neolbeotteon

Want	Can
—	넓을 수 있어요
	neolbeul su isseoyo

Don't (Imperative)	Whether or not		
—	넓은지	넓었는지	넓을지
	neolbeunji	neolbeonneunji	neolbeuljji

(tell someone) that	(tell someone) to
넓다고	넓으라고
neolttago	neolbeurago

Sample Sentences

1. 현우 씨는 그 방이 너무 넓다고 싫대요.
   Hyunwoo said he didn't like the room because it's too wide.

2. 저는 넓은 방이 좋아요.
   I like big rooms.

3. 방이 굉장히 넓어요.
   The room is very wide.

4. 얼마나 넓은지 물어봤어요?
   Did you ask them how wide it is?

5. 이번에 이사가는 집은 얼마나 넓어요?
   How big is the house you are moving to?

Quiz

1. 수지 씨는 TV 화면 너무 (   ) 싫대요.
   Suji said she didn't like the TV screen because it's too wide.

2. 중기 씨는 (   ) 도로가 좋대요.
   Joon-ki said he likes wide roads.

3. 어제 산 핸드폰은 화면이 얼마나 (   )?
   How big is the screen of the phone you bought yesterday?

49

떠나다

to leave

The Korean Verbs Guide - vol.2

Conceptual

Present	Past	Future / Guessing	Present Progressive
떠나요	떠났어요	떠날 거예요	떠나고 있어요
tteonayo	tteonasseoyo	tteonal geoyeyo	tteonago isseoyo

Imperative

떠나세요	떠나요	떠나	떠나라
tteonaseyo	tteonayo	tteona	tteonara

Modifier

떠난	떠나는	떠날	떠나던	떠났던
tteonan	tteonaneun	tteonal	tteonadeon	tteonattteon

Want	Can
떠나고 싶어요	떠날 수 있어요
tteonago sipeyo	tteonal su isseoyo

Don't (Imperative)	Whether or not		
떠나지 마세요	떠나는지	떠났는지	떠날지
tteonaji maseyo	tteonaneunji	tteonanneunji	tteonaljji

(tell someone) that	(tell someone) to
떠난다고	떠나라고
tteonandago	tteonarago

Sample Sentences

1. 지금 당장 떠나세요.
   Please leave right now.

2. 이제 떠날 시간이에요.
   It is time to leave now.

3. 지금 당장 떠날 수 있어요.
   I can leave right now.

4. 미영 씨가 언제 떠났는지 알아요?
   Do you know when Miyeong left?

5. 저 혼자 두고 떠나지 마세요.
   Please don't leave me by myself and go (alone).

Quiz

1. 엄마가 오시면 같이 (   ).
   When your mom comes, leave with her, please.

2. 저는 언제든지 (   ).
   I can leave any time.

3. 아직 (   ).
   Please don't leave yet.

The Korean Verbs Guide - vol.2

Answers :
1. 떠나세요 or 떠나렴 / 2. 떠날 수 있어요 / 3. 떠나지 마세요

때리다

to hit (someone)

Conjugation

Present	Past	Future / Guessing	Present Progressive
때려요	때렸어요	때릴 거예요	때리고 있어요
ttaeryeoyo	ttaeryeosseoyo	ttaeril geoyeyo	ttaerigo isseoyo

Imperative

때리세요	때려요	때려	때려라
ttaeriseyo	ttaeryeoyo	ttaeryeo	ttaeryeora

Modifier

때린	때리는	때릴	때리던	때렸던
ttaerin	ttaerineun	ttaeril	ttaerideon	ttaeryeotteon

Want	Can
때리고 싶어요	때릴 수 있어요
ttaerigo sipeoyo	ttaeril su isseoyo

Don't (Imperative)	Whether or not		
때리지 마세요	때리는지	때렸는지	때릴지
ttaeriji maseyo	ttaerineunji	ttaeryeonneunji	ttaeriljji

(tell someone) that	(tell someone) to
때린다고	때리라고
ttaerindago	ttaerirago

Sample Sentences

Track
65

1. 자꾸 그런 말 하면 때릴 거예요.
   If you keep saying things like that, I am going to hit you.

2. 누가 때렸는지 말해 보세요.
   Please tell me who hit you.

3. 방금 나 때린 사람 나와.
   Whoever just hit me, come forward.

4. 누가 그렇게 세게 때리라고 했어요?
   Who said to hit (me) that hard?

5. 동생이 저 때렸어요.
   My little sister hit me.

Quiz

1. 자꾸 저 놀리면 진짜로 (   ).
   If you keep teasing me, I'm really going to hit you.

2. 누가 (   ) 알아요?
   Do you know who hit you?

3. 아까 제 등 (   ) 사람 누군지 알아요?
   Do you know the person who hit me in the back?

일어나다

to wake up;
to get up

Conjugation

일어나다

Present	Past	Future / Guessing	Present Progressive
일어나요	일어났어요	일어날 거예요	일어나고 있어요
ireonayo	ireonasseoyo	ireonal geoyeyo	ireonago isseoyo

Imperative

일어나세요	일어나요	일어나	일어나라
ireonaseyo	ireonayo	ireona	ireonara

Modifier

일어난	일어나는	일어날	일어나던	일어났던
ireonan	ireonaneun	ireonal	ireonadeon	ireonattteon

Want

일어나고 싶어요
ireonago sipeoyo

Can

일어날 수 있어요
ireonal su isseoyo

Don't (Imperative)

일어나지 마세요
ireonaji maseyo

Whether or not

일어나는지	일어났는지	일어날지
ireonaneunji	ireonanneunji	ireonaljji

(tell someone) that

일어난다고
ireonandago

(tell someone) to

일어나라고
ireonarago

Sample Sentences

1. 저는 매일 아침 8시에 일어나요.
   I wake up every day at 8 in the morning.

2. 저는 아침에 일어나는 시간이 매일 달라요.
   I wake up at a different time every day.

3. 내일 몇 시에 일어날지 알려 주시면 아침 식사를 준비해 놓을게요.
   If you tell me what time you plan on waking up in the morning, I will
   make sure breakfast is prepared.

4. 깨워 주지 않으셔도 저 혼자 일어날 수 있어요.
   Even if you don't wake me up, I can wake up by myself.

5. 아침 일찍 일어나는 습관을 기르고 싶어요.
   I want get in the habit of waking up early in the morning.

Quiz

1. 저희 가족은 모두 매일 아침 6시에 (   ).
   Everyone in my family wakes up every day at 6 in the morning.

2. 제 동생은 주말에도 아침에 (   ) 시간이 매일 똑같아요.
   My younger sister wakes up at the same time every day, even on the
   weekends.

3. 알람 시계가 있어서 혼자 (   ).
   Because I have an alarmclock, I can wake up by myself.

Answers :
1. 일어나요 / 2. 일어나는 / 3. 일어날 수 있어요

The Korean Verbs Guide - vol.2

늦다
to be late

Conjugation

늦다
neut-tta

Present	Past	Future / Guessing	Present Progressive
늦어요	늦었어요	늦을 거예요	—
neujeoyo	neujeosseoyo	neujeul geoyeyo	

Imperative

—	—	—	—

Modifier

늦은	늦는	늦을	늦던	늦었던
neujeun	neunneun	neujeul	neuttteon	neujeottteon

Want	Can
—	늦을 수 있어요
	neujeul su isseoyo

Don't (Imperative)	Whether or not		
늦지 마세요	늦는지	늦었는지	늦을지
neutjji maseyo	neunneunji	neojeonneunji	neujeuljji

(tell someone) that	(tell someone) to
늦는다고	늦으라고
neunneundago	neujeurago

The Korean Verbs Guide - vol.2

Sample Sentences

Track
67

1. 내일은 절대 늦지 마세요.
   Please don't be late tomorrow.

2. 내일 늦는 사람은 벌금 내야 돼요.
   People who are late tomorrow have to pay a fine.

3. 지수 씨 오늘도 1시간 늦는다고 했어요.
   Jisoo said she was going to be an hour late again today.

4. 늦잠 자서 늦었어요.
   I was late because I overslept.

5. 저 오늘 좀 늦을 거예요.
   I'm going to be a little late today.

Quiz

1. 앞으로는 절대 (   ).
   From now on please don't be late.

2. 진영 씨 오늘도 (   ) 했어요?
   Did Jin-yeong say he was going to be late again today?

3. 차가 막혀서 (   ).
   I was late because there was a traffic jam.

Answers :
1. 늦지 마세요 / 2. 늦는다고 / 3. 늦었어요

61

제 아내는 취미로
허브를 길러요

My wife grows herbs as a hobby.

기르다

to grow; to raise

Conjugation

Present	Past	Future / Guessing	Present Progressive
길러요	길렀어요	기를 거예요	기르고 있어요
gilleoyo	gilleosseoyo	gireul geoyeyo	gireugo isseoyo

Imperative

기르세요	길러요	길러	길러라
gireuseyo	gilleoyo	gilleo	gilleora

Modifier

기른	기르는	기를	기르던	길렀던
gireun	gireuneun	gireul	gireudeon	gilleottteon

Want / Can

Want	Can
기르고 싶어요	기를 수 있어요
gireugo sipeoyo	gireul su isseoyo

Don't (Imperative) / Whether or not

Don't (Imperative)	Whether or not		
기르지 마세요	기르는지	길렀는지	기를지
gireuji maseyo	gireuneunji	gilleonneunji	gireuljji

(tell someone) that / (tell someone) to

(tell someone) that	(tell someone) to
기른다고	기르라고
gireundago	gireurago

Sample Sentences

1. 당분간 머리 안 자르고 기를 거예요.
   I'm going to stop cutting my hair for a while and just let my hair grow.

2. 이 당근을 정말 집에서 길렀어요?
   Did you really grow this carrot at home?

3. 제가 기르던 난초가 죽었어요.
   The orchids I was growing died.

4. 머리를 허리까지 기르고 싶어요.
   I want to grow my hair all the way down to my waist.

5. 제 아내는 취미로 허브를 길러요.
   My wife grows herbs as a hobby.

Quiz

1. 이렇게 많은 꽃들을 혼자 (   )?
   Did you grow these many flowers all by yourself?

2. 작년부터 동생이 (   ) 선인장이 죽었어요.
   The cactus my little sister was growing died.

3. 제 친구는 집에서 방울 토마토를 (   ).
   A friend of mine grows cherry tomatoes at his house.

Answers :
1. 길렀어요 / 2. 기르던 / 3. 길러요

65

싸우다

to fight, to argue

Conjugation

Present	Past	Future / Guessing	Present Progressive
싸워요	싸웠어요	싸울 거예요	싸우고 있어요
ssawoyo	ssawosseoyo	ssaul geoyeyo	ssaugo isseoyo

Imperative

싸우세요	싸워요	싸워	싸워라
ssauseyo	ssawoyo	ssawo	ssawora

Modifier

싸운	싸우는	싸울	싸우던	싸웠던
ssaun	ssauneun	ssaul	ssaudeon	ssawottteon

Want	Can
싸우고 싶어요	싸울 수 있어요
ssaugo sipeoyo	ssaul su isseoyo

Don't (Imperative)	Whether or not		
싸우지 마세요	싸우는지	싸웠는지	싸울지
ssauji maseyo	ssauneunji	ssawonneunji	ssauljji

(tell someone) that	(tell someone) to
싸운다고	싸우라고
ssaundago	ssaurago

Sample Sentences

1. 옆 집에서 싸우는 소리가 들렸어요.
   I heard people fighting next door.

2. 그 두 사람은 자주 싸운다고 들었어요.
   I heard those two people fight a lot.

3. 밖에서 누가 지금 싸우고 있어요.
   Someone is fighting outside right now.

4. 어릴 때 저랑 자주 싸웠던 친구예요.
   He is a friend who I used to fight a lot with when we were younger.

5. 아이들끼리 놀다 보면 싸울 수 있어요.
   Sometimes kids can fight when they play with each other.

Quiz

1. 밖에서 (   ) 소리 들려요?
   Do you hear people fighting outside?

2. 지금 안에서 누가 (   )?
   Is someone fighting inside now?

3. 부부도 가끔 (   ).
   Sometimes couples can fight with each other.

Answers :
1. 싸우는 / 2. 싸우고 있어요 / 3. 싸울 수 있어요

The Korean Verbs Guide - vol.2

싸다
to be cheap,
to be inexpensive

Conjugation

Present	Past	Future / Guessing	Present Progressive
싸요	쌌어요	쌀 거예요	—
ssayo	ssasseoyo	ssal geoyeyo	

		Imperative		
—	—	—	—

		Modifier		
싼	—	쌀	싸던	쌌던
ssan		ssal	ssadeon	ssattteon

Want	Can
—	쌀 수 있어요
	ssal su isseoyo

Don't (Imperative)	Whether or not		
—	싼지	쌌는지	쌀지
	ssanji	ssanneunji	ssaljji

(tell someone) that	(tell someone) to
싸다고	—
ssadago	

Sample Sentences

1. 그렇게 싸요?
   Is it that cheap?

2. 과일이 이렇게 쌀지 몰랐어요.
   I didn't know fruits would be so cheap here.

3. 작년에는 비쌌는데 올해는 쌀 거예요.
   It was expensive last year, but it will be cheap this year.

4. 저한테는 이게 제일 싸다고 거짓말 했어요.
   They lied and told me that this was the cheapest one.

5. 싼 볼펜을 샀더니 금방 고장 났어요.
   I bought a cheap pen and it broke quickly.

Quiz

1. 왜 그렇게 (   )?
   Why is it that cheap?

2. 그 사람이 저한테 그게 여기서 제일 (   ) 말해줬어요.
   He told me that was the cheapest here.

3. (   ) 핸드폰을 샀는데 나쁘지 않아요.
   I bought a cheap cell phone and it's not bad.

Answers :
1. 싸요 / 2. 싸다고 / 3. 싼

71

비싸다
to be expensive

Conjugation

Present	Past	Future / Guessing	Present Progressive
비싸요	비쌌어요	비쌀 거예요	—
bissayo	bissasseoyo	bissal geoyeyo	

Imperative

—	—	—	—

Modifier

비싼	—	비쌀	비싸던	비쌌던
bissan		bissal	bissadeon	bissattteon

Want	Can
—	비쌀 수 있어요
	bissal su isseoyo

Don't (Imperative)	Whether or not		
—	비싼지	비쌌는지	비쌀지
	bissanji	bissanneunji	bissaljji

(tell someone) that	(tell someone) to
비싸다고	—
bissadago	

Sample Sentences

1. 왜 이렇게 비싸요?
   Why is it so expensive?

2. 영국은 물가가 비싸다고 들었어요.
   I heard that prices are expensive in the U.K.

3. 비싼 물건이라고 다 좋은 건 아니에요.
   Just because it's expensive doesn't mean that it's good.

4. 수공예 제품이라 비쌀 수 있어요.
   Since it's handmade, it can be expensive.

5. 수입한 물건이라 비쌀 거예요.
   Since it's an imported item, it is going to be expensive.

Quiz

1. 유키에 씨가 일본은 물가가 (   ) 했어요.
   Yukie said prices are expensive in Japan.

2. 유명한 디자이너가 디자인한 거라 (   ).
   Since a famous designer designed it, it can be expensive.

3. 한정판이라 (   ).
   Since it's a limited-edition, it is going to be expensive.

Answers :
1. 비싸다고 / 2. 비쌀 수 있어요 / 3. 비쌀 거예요

제 사진 찍지 마세요.

Don't take my pictures, please.

찍다
to take (a photo)

Conjugation

Present	Past	Future / Guessing	Present Progressive
찍어요	찍었어요	찍을 거예요	찍고 있어요
jjigeoyo	jjigeosseoyo	jjigeul geoyeyo	jjikkko isseoyo

Imperative

찍으세요	찍어요	찍어	찍어라
jjigeuseyo	jjigeoyo	jjigeo	jjigeora

Modifier

찍은	찍는	찍을	찍던	찍었던
jjigeun	jjingneun	jjigeul	jjik-tteon	jjigeottteon

Want

찍고 싶어요
jjikkko sipeoyo

Can

찍을 수 있어요
jjigeul su isseoyo

Don't (Imperative)

찍지 마세요
jjikjji maseyo

Whether or not

찍는지	찍었는지	찍을지
jjingneunji	jjigeonneunji	jjigeuljji

(tell someone) that

찍는다고
jjingneundago

(tell someone) to

찍으라고
jjigeurago

Sample Sentences

1. 새 카메라 사면 사진 많이 찍을 거예요.
   If I buy a new camera, I will take a lot of pictures.

2. 저도 비싼 카메라 있으면 사진 잘 찍을 수 있어요.
   If I had an expensive camera, I could take good pictures.

3. 제 사진 찍지 마세요.
   Don't take my pictures, please.

4. 제가 찍은 사진 어때요?
   How is the photo I took?

5. 같이 사진 찍어요.
   Let's take a photo together.

Quiz

1. 이번에 여행 가면 사진 많이 (   ).
   While I am on my trip this time, I will take a lot of pictures.

2. 박물관 안에서 사진 (   ).
   Don't take any pictures inside the museum, please.

3. 내일 웃긴 사진 (   ).
   Let's take funny photos tomorrow.

Answers :
1. 찍을 거예요 / 2. 찍지 마세요 / 3. 찍어요

The Korean Verbs Guide - vol.2

졸다
to doze off

Conjugation

Present	Past	Future / Guessing	Present Progressive
졸아요	졸았어요	졸 거예요	졸고 있어요
jorayo	jorasseoyo	jol geoyeyo	jolgo isseoyo

Imperative

조세요	졸아요	졸아	졸아라
joseyo	jorayo	jora	jorara

Modifier

존	조는	졸	졸던	졸았던
jon	joneun	jol	joldeon	jorattteon

Want	Can
졸고 싶어요	졸 수 있어요
jolgo sipeoyo	jol su isseyo

Don't (Imperative)	Whether or not		
졸지 마세요	조는지	졸았는지	졸지
jolji maseyo	joneunji	joranneunji	jolji

(tell someone) that	(tell someone) to
존다고	—
jondago	

Sample Sentences

1. 오늘 시험 보다가 졸았어요.
   I dozed off while taking my exam today.

2. 운전 중에는 절대로 졸지 마세요.
   Please never doze off while you are driving.

3. 왜 자꾸 졸아요?
   Why do you keep dozing off?

4. 저도 그 영화 보면서 졸았던 기억이 있어요.
   I also remember dozing off while watching that movie.

5. 지금 교실 안에 조는 사람이 8명이나 돼요.
   There are about eight people dozing off in the classroom right now.

Quiz

1. 아까 밥 먹다가 (   ).
   I dozed off while I was eating earlier today.

2. 걸을 때는 (   ).
   Please don't doze off while you are walking.

3. 사무실 안에 (   ) 사람이 한 명도 없어요.
   There is no one dozing off in the office.

Answers :
1. 졸았어요 / 2. 졸지 마세요 / 3. 조는

쉬다

to rest
to take time off

Conjugation

Present	Past	Future / Guessing	Present Progressive
쉬어요	쉬었어요	쉴 거예요	쉬고 있어요
swieoyo	swieosseoyo	swil geoyeyo	swigo isseoyo

Imperative

쉬세요	쉬어요	쉬어	쉬어라
swiseyo	swieoyo	swieo	swieora

Modifier

쉰	쉬는	쉴	쉬던	쉬었던
swin	swineun	swil	swideon	swieottteon

Want

쉬고 싶어요
swigo sipeoyo

Can

쉴 수 있어요
swil su isseoyo

Don't (Imperative)

쉬지 마세요
swiji maseyo

Whether or not

쉬는지	쉬었는지	쉴지
swineunji	swieonneunji	swiljji

(tell someone) that

쉰다고
swindago

(tell someone) to

쉬라고
swirago

Sample Sentences

1. 푹 쉬었어요?
   Have you rested up?

2. 쉬는 날이 언제예요?
   When is your day off?

3. 지금은 일 안 하고 쉬고 있어요.
   I am taking time off and not working now.

4. 주말에는 쉬고 싶어요.
   I want to rest on the weekend.

5. 이거 다 하면 쉴 수 있어요.
   If I finish this, I can rest.

Quiz

1. 주연 씨, 어제 (   )?
   Jooyeon, did you have a day off yesterday?

2. (   ) 시간에 잠깐 밖에 나갈까요?
   Shall we go out for a minute during the break?

3. 오늘 시험 끝나서 내일부터 (   ).
   The exams ended today, so I can rest starting tomorrow.

Answers :
1. 쉬었어요 / 2. 쉬는 / 3. 쉴 수 있어요

The Korean Verbs Guide - vol.2

크다

to be big,
to be large

Conjugation

Present	Past	Future / Guessing	Present Progressive
커요	컸어요	클 거예요	—
keoyo	keosseoyo	keul geoyeyo	

Imperative

—	—	—	—

Modifier

큰	—	클	크던	컸던
keun		keul	keudeon	keottteon

Want	Can
—	클 수 있어요
	keul su isseyo

Don't (Imperative)	Whether or not		
—	큰지	컸는지	클지
	keunji	keonneunji	keuljji

(tell someone) that	(tell someone) to
크다고	—
keudago	

Sample Sentences

1. 얼마나 컸는지 기억나요?
   Do you remember how big it was?

2. 농구공보다 커요.
   It is bigger than a basketball.

3. 그 가방보다 클 거예요.
   It will be bigger than that bag.

4. 얼마나 큰지 알아요?
   Do you know how big it is?

5. 크다고 들었는데 별로 안 컸어요.
   I heard it was big, but it wasn't that big.

Quiz

1. 수박보다 훨씬 (   ).
   It's a lot bigger than a watermelon.

2. 저 산보다는 안 (   ).
   It won't be bigger than that mountain.

3. 그게 얼마나 (   ) 아는 사람 있어요?
   Is there anyone who knows how big it is?

과자가 너무 작아서 다 먹고
나서도 배가 고팠어요.

Since the cookies were too small, even after I ate them all,
I still felt hungry.

작다
to be small

Conjugation

Present	Past	Future / Guessing	Present Progressive
작아요	작았어요	작을 거예요	—
jagayo	jagasseoyo	jageul geoyeyo	

Imperative

—	—	—	—

Modifier

작은	—	작을	작던	작았던
jageun		jageul	jaktteon	jagattteon

Want	Can
—	작을 수 있어요
	jageul su isseoyo

Don't (Imperative)	Whether or not		
—	작은지	작았는지	작을지
	jageunji	jaganneunji	jageuljji

(tell someone) that	(tell someone) to
작다고	—
jakttago	

Sample Sentences

1. 이 신발은 저한테는 좀 작아요.
   These shoes are a little small for me.

2. 거기 그 작은 방은 제 동생 방이에요.
   That small room over there is my little brother's room.

3. 작년에 작았던 옷이 살을 뺐더니 이제는 잘 맞아요.
   The clothes that were small on me last year now fit me well because I lost weight.

4. 치마가 작은지 안 작은지 볼 수 있게 입어 보세요.
   Please try this skirt on so that I can see if it's small or not (for you).

5. 이 바지는 제가 입어 봤을 때는 좀 작았어요.
   When I tried these pants on, they were a little small.

Quiz

1. 그 자켓은 제가 입기에는 좀 (   ).
   That jacket is a little small for me to wear.

2. 여기 (   ) 방은 누구 방이에요?
   Whose room is this small room?

3. 모자가 (   ) 안 (   ) 써 보기 전에는 몰라요.
   You don't know if a hat is small or not until you wear it.

졸리다

to be sleepy, to feel
sleepy; to be so boring
that it makes one sleepy

Present	Past	Future / Guessing	Present Progressive
졸려요	졸렸어요	졸릴 거예요	—
jollyeoyo	jollyeosseoyo	jollil geoyeyo	

Imperative

—	—	—	—

Modifier

졸린	—	졸릴	졸리던	졸렸던
jollin		jollil	jollideon	jollyeotteon

Want	Can
—	졸릴 수 있어요
	jollil su isseoyo

Don't (Imperative)	Whether or not		
—	졸린지	졸렸는지	졸릴지
	jollinji	jollyeonneunji	jolliljji

(tell someone) that	(tell someone) to
졸리다고	—
jollidago	

Sample Sentences

1. 어제 강의 정말 졸렸어요.
   Yesterday's lecture was really boring (and made me sleepy).

2. 밥 먹고 나면 누구나 졸려요.
   Everyone feels sleepy after they have a meal.

3. 어젯밤에 뭐 했길래 그렇게 졸린 눈을 하고 있어요?
   What did you do last night that made your eyes look so sleepy?

4. 영화 보러 간 친구가 졸리다고 문자를 보냈어요.
   My friend, who went to see a movie, texted me and said he's sleepy.

5. 아까 졸렸는데 지금은 괜찮아요.
   I was sleepy before, but I'm okay now.

Quiz

1. 오늘 회의 정말 (   ).
   Today's meeting was really boring (and made me sleepy).

2. 저는 밥 먹고 나면 항상 (   ).
   I always feel sleepy after I have a meal.

3. 어제는 하루종일 (   ) 어젯밤에 10시간 잤더니
   오늘은 괜찮아요.
   I was sleepy all day long yesterday, but after sleeping for ten
   hours last night, I'm okay now.

피하다

to avoid, to dodge,
to duck (down)

Conjugation

Present	Past	Future / Guessing	Present Progressive
피해요	피했어요	피할 거예요	피하고 있어요
pihaeyo	pihaesseoyo	pihal geoyeyo	pihago isseoyo

Imperative

피하세요	피해요	피해	피해라
pihaseyo	pihaeyo	pihae	pihaera

Modifier

피한	피하는	피할	피하던	피했던
pihan	pihaneun	pihal	pihadeon	pihaettteon

Want

피하고 싶어요
pihago sipeoyo

Can

피할 수 있어요
pihal su isseoyo

Don't (Imperative)

피하지 마세요
pihaji maseyo

Whether or not

피하는지	피했는지	피할지
pihaneunji	pihaenneunji	pihaljji

(tell someone) that

피한다고
pihandago

(tell someone) to

피하라고
piharago

Sample Sentences

1. 저 피하는 이유가 뭐예요?
   What's the reason you are avoiding me?

2. 될 수 있으면 그런 상황은 피하고 싶어요.
   I want to avoid that kind of situation as much as I can.

3. 살 빼고 싶으면 패스트 푸드는 피하세요.
   If you want to lose weight, please avoid junk food.

4. 그 사람 만나는 게 조금 불편해서 일부러 피했어요.
   I felt uncomfortable meeting him, so I avoided him.

5. 꼭 하고 싶은 말이 있으니까 오늘은 저를 피하지 마세요.
   I have something I really want to tell you, so please don't avoid me.

Quiz

1. 유리 씨를 (   ) 이유를 말해 주세요.
   Please tell me the reason why you are avoiding Yuri.

2. 오늘 밤에 악몽 꾸고 싶지 않으면 공포 영화는 (   ).
   If you don't want to have a nightmare tonight, please avoid a horror
   movie.

3. 전해주고 싶은 게 있으니까 이따가 저 (   ).
   I have something I want to give you, so please don't avoid me later.

화내다

to get angry;
to yell (at someone
out of anger)

Conjugation

Present	Past	Future / Guessing	Present Progressive
화내요	화냈어요	화낼 거예요	화내고 있어요
hwanaeyo	hwanaesseoyo	hwanael geoyeyo	hwanaego isseoyo

Imperative

화내세요	화내요	화내	화내라
hwanaeseyo	hwanaeyo	hwanae	hwanaera

Modifier

화낸	화내는	화낼	화내던	화냈던
hwanaen	hwanaeneun	hwanael	hwanaedeon	hwanaettteon

Want	Can
화내고 싶어요	화낼 수 있어요
hwanaego sipeoyo	hwanael su isseoyo

Don't (Imperative)	Whether or not		
화내지 마세요	화내는지	화냈는지	화낼지
hwanaeji maseyo	hwanaeneunji	hwanaennuenji	hwanaeljji

(tell someone) that	(tell someone) to
화낸다고	화내라고
hwanaendago	hwanaerago

Sample Sentences

1. 제가 그런 거 아니니까 저한테 화내지 마세요.
   I didn't do it, so please don't be mad at me.

2. 그런 상황에서는 누구나 화낼 수 있어요.
   In that kind of situation, anyone can get angry.

3. 너무 화가 나서 저도 모르게 동생한테 화냈어요.
   I was so angry that I yelled at my little brother unintentionally.

4. 성민 씨가 우리한테 화낸 이유를 이제 알았어요.
   Now I know why Seongmin yelled at us.

5. 저는 민규 씨한테 화낸 기억이 없어요.
   I don't remember yelling at Min-gyu.

Quiz

1. 저하고는 관계 없는 일이니까 저한테 (   ).
   It has nothing to do with me, so please don't be mad at me.

2. 어제는 동생 때문에 화가 나서 동생한테 (   ).
   I was angry because of my little sister, so I yelled at her.

3. 지숙 씨가 (   ) 이유 알아요?
   Do you know why Jisook yelled at us?

Answers :
1. 화내지 마세요. / 2. 화냈어요. / 3. 화낸

아프다

to be sick, to feel sick; to hurt

Conjugation

Present	Past	Future / Guessing	Present Progressive
아파요	아팠어요	아플 거예요	—
apayo	apasseoyo	apeul geoyeyo	

Imperative

—	—	—	—

Modifier

아픈	—	아플	아프던	아팠던
apeun		apeul	apeudeon	apattteon

Want	Can
—	아플 수 있어요
	apeul su isseoyo

Don't (Imperative)		Whether or not		
아프지 마세요		아픈지	아팠는지	아플지
apeuji maseyo		apeunji	apanneunji	apeuljji

(tell someone) that	(tell someone) to
아프다고	—
apeudago	

Sample Sentences

1. 동생이 어디가 아픈지 물어 봐.
   Ask your little brother where it hurts.

2. 조금 아플 거예요.
   It will hurt a little.

3. 정말 아팠어요.
   It really hurt.

4. 아픈 사람은 방에 가서 쉬어요.
   People who are sick, go to the room and get some rest.

5. 아프다고 말을 안 해서 아픈지 몰랐어요.
   Since you didn't tell me you were sick, I didn't know you were sick.

Quiz

1. 별로 안 (   ).
   It won't hurt that much.

2. 별로 안 (   ).
   It didn't hurt much.

3. (   ) 사람은 병원에 가세요.
   People who are sick, please make sure to go see a doctor.

오토바이는 위험하니까
타지 마세요.

Motorcycles are dangerous so don't ride them.

타다

(transportation) to take,
to ride, to get on

Conjugation

Present	Past	Future / Guessing	Present Progressive
타요	탔어요	탈 거예요	타고 있어요
tayo	tasseoyo	tal geoyeyo	tago isseoyo

Imperative

타세요	타요	타	타라
taseyo	tayo	ta	tara

Modifier

탄	타는	탈	타던	탔던
tan	taneun	tal	tadeon	tattteon

Want	Can
타고 싶어요	탈 수 있어요
tago sipeoyo	tal su isseoyo

Don't (Imperative)	Whether or not		
타지 마세요	타는지	탔는지	탈지
taji maseyo	taneunji	tanneunji	talji

(tell someone) that	(tell someone) to
탄다고	타라고
tandago	tarago

Sample Sentences

1. 내일 제가 탈 기차는 KTX보다 느려요.
   The train I will be riding tomorrow is slower than the KTX.

2. 제가 어제 탔던 자전거는 지용 씨 거예요.
   The bicycle I rode yesterday was Jiyong's.

3. 오토바이는 위험하니까 타지 마세요.
   Motorcycles are dangerous, so don't ride them.

4. 지하철 말고 버스 탈 거예요.
   I'm going to take the bus, not the subway.

5. 제가 탄 버스가 갑자기 멈췄어요.
   The bus I'm riding in, suddenly stopped.

Quiz

1. 제가 다음 달에 (   ) 비행기는 다른 비행기들보다 커요.
   The airplane I'll be riding next month is bigger than other planes.

2. 위험하니까 혼자서는 (   ).
   It's dangerous, so don't ride it alone.

3. 우리 지난 주에 (   ) 자동차 이름이 뭐예요?
   What is the name of the car we rode last week?

느끼다

to feel

Conjugation

Present	Past	Future / Guessing	Present Progressive
느껴요	느꼈어요	느낄 거예요	느끼고 있어요
neukkyeoyo	neukkyeosseoyo	neukkil geoyeyo	neukkigo isseoyo

Imperative

느끼세요	느껴요	느껴	느껴라
neukkiseyo	neukkyeyo	neukkyeo	neukkyeora

Modifier

느낀	느끼는	느낄	느끼던	느꼈던
neukkin	neukkineun	neukkil	neukkideon	neukkyeottteon

Want

느끼고 싶어요

neukkigo sipeoyo

Can

느낄 수 있어요

neukkil su isseoyo

Don't (Imperative)

느끼지 마세요

neukkiji maseyo

Whether or not

느끼는지	느꼈는지	느낄지
neukkineunji	neukkyeonneunji	neukkiljji

(tell someone) that

느낀다고

neukkindago

(tell someone) to

느끼라고

neukkirago

Sample Sentences

1. 이 영화를 보고 뭘 느꼈어요?
   What did you feel after you saw the movie?

2. 제가 느낀 감정을 솔직하게 이야기 할게요.
   I'll tell you how I honestly felt (about it).

3. 출근 안 하고 여행 가고 싶은 충동을 자주 느껴요.
   I often feel the urge not to go to work, but rather go on a trip.

4. 저도 그런 따뜻한 감정을 느끼고 싶어요.
   I want to feel that kind of warm feeling, too.

5. 오늘 그 두 사람 사이가 어색하다고 느낀 사람 저 말고 또 있어요?
   Is there anyone else who felt like it was awkward between those two people?

Quiz

1. 그 책을 읽고 뭘 (   )?
   How did you feel after you read that book?

2. 학교 안 가고 집에서 쉬고 싶은 충동을 자주 (   ).
   I often feel the urge not to go to school but to just rest at home.

3. 그 두 사람 사이에 뭔가 있다고 (   ) 사람?
   Who felt like there was something between those two people?

Answers :
1. 느꼈어요 / 2. 느껴요 / 3. 느낀

죽다
to die

Conjugation

Present	Past	Future / Guessing	Present Progressive
죽어요	죽었어요	죽을 거예요	죽고 있어요
jugeoyo	jugeosseoyo	jugeul geoyeyo	jukkko isseoyo

Imperative

죽으세요	죽어요	죽어	죽어라
jugeuseyo	jugeoyo	jugeo	jugeora

Modifier

죽은	죽는	죽을	죽던	죽었던
jugeun	jungneun	jugeul	juktteon	jugeottteon

Want	Can
죽고 싶어요	죽을 수 있어요
jukkko sipeoyo	jugeul su isseoyo

Don't (Imperative)	Whether or not		
죽지 마세요	죽는지	죽었는지	죽을지
jukjji maseyo	jungneunji	jugeonneunji	jugeuljji

(tell someone) that	(tell someone) to
죽는다고	죽으라고
jungneundago	jugeurago

Sample Sentences

1. 저는 이 영화에서 누가 죽는지 알고 있어요.
   I know who dies in this film.

2. 저는 사람이 죽는 게임은 싫어해요.
   I don't like games where people die (in the game).

3. 죽은 사람이 자꾸 꿈에 나타난다고요?
   Are you saying a dead person keeps appearing in your dream?

4. 제가 어릴 때 기르던 고양이는 제가 15살 때 죽었어요.
   The cat I had when I was little died when I was 15.

5. 물을 안 주면 꽃이 금방 죽을 거예요.
   If you don't water the flower, it will die soon

Quiz

1. 이 소설에서 누가 (   ) 알아요?
   Do you know who dies in this novel?

2. 저희 집 강아지가 최근에 (   ).
   My dog died recently.

3. 먹이를 안 주면 금붕어가 (   ).
   If you don't feed the gold fish, they will die.

Answers :
1. 죽는지 / 2. 죽었어요 / 3. 죽을 거예요

113

느리다
to be slow

Conjugation

Present	Past	Future / Guessing	Present Progressive
느려요	느렸어요	느릴 거예요	—
neuryeoyo	neuryeosseoyo	neuril geoyeyo	

Imperative

—	—	—	—

Modifier

느린	—	느릴	느리던	느렸던
neurin		neuril	neurideon	neuryeotteon

Want	Can
—	느릴 수 있어요
	neuril su isseoyo

Don't (Imperative)	Whether or not		
—	느린지	느렸는지	느릴지
	neurinji	neuryeonneunji	neuriljji

(tell someone) that	(tell someone) to
느리다고	—
neuridago	

Sample Sentences

1. 느린 컴퓨터로 일하려니 효율이 떨어져요.
   I'm trying to work with a slow computer and it's really ineffective.

2. 얼마나 느린지 상상이 안 돼요.
   I can't imagine how slow it is.

3. 컴퓨터를 새로 사니까 제 옛날 컴퓨터가 얼마나 느렸는지 이제 알겠어요.
   Now that I've bought a new computer, I realize how slow my old computer was.

4. 여기는 인터넷 속도가 조금 느려요.
   The internet is a bit slow here.

5. 제 기억에는 정말 느렸어요.
   As far as I remember, it was very slow.

Quiz

1. (   ) 컴퓨터로 게임을 하려니 재미가 없어요.
   I'm trying to play a game on a slow computer and it's not really fun.

2. 얼마나 (   ) 알아요?
   Do you know how slow it is?

3. 저희 집은 인터넷 속도가 별로 안 (   ).
   The internet is not that slow in my house.

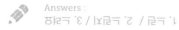

Answers :
1. 느린 / 2. 느린지 / 3. 느려요

The Korean Verbs Guide - vol.2

같은 색깔의 버스가 많아요.

There are many buses with the same color.

같다

to be the same

Conjugation

Present	Past	Future / Guessing	Present Progressive
같아요	같았어요	같을 거예요	—
gatayo	gatasseoyo	gateul geoyeyo	

Imperative

—	—	—	—

Modifier

같은	—	같을	같던	같았던
gateun		gateul	gattteon	gatattteon

Want · Can

Want	Can
—	같을 수 있어요
	gateul su isseoyo

Don't (Imperative) · Whether or not

Don't (Imperative)	Whether or not		
—	같은지	같았는지	같을지
	gateunji	gatanneunji	gateuljji

(tell someone) that · (tell someone) to

(tell someone) that	(tell someone) to
같다고	—
gatttago	

Sample Sentences

1. 가격이 같은지 물어봐 주세요.
   Please ask if the price is the same.

2. 내일 같은 시간, 같은 장소에서 봐요.
   I will see you tomorrow at the same place, same time.

3. 저랑 나이가 같다고요?
   You said we are the same age?

4. 저랑 지은 씨는 몸무게는 다른데 키는 같아요.
   Jieun and I have different weights, but our height is the same.

5. 같았는지 달랐는지 기억이 안 나요.
   I don't remember if it was the same or if it was different.

Quiz

1. 시간도 (   ) 알려주세요.
   Please let me know if the time is the same, too.

2. 다음 주에도 (   ) 시간에 볼까요?
   Should we meet up at the same time next week, too?

3. (   ) 달랐는지 말해 주세요.
   Please tell me if it was the same or if it was different.

Answers :
1. 같은지 / 2. 같은 / 3. 같았는지

The Korean Verbs Guide - vol.2

나가다

to go out,
to get out

Conjugation

Present	Past	Future / Guessing	Present Progressive
나가요	나갔어요	나갈 거예요	나가고 있어요
nagayo	nagasseoyo	nagal geoyeyo	nagago isseoyo

Imperative

나가세요	나가요	나가	나가라
nagaseyo	nagayo	naga	nagara

Modifier

나간	나가는	나갈	나가던	나갔던
nagan	naganeun	nagal	nagadeon	nagattteon

Want / Can

Want	Can
나가고 싶어요	나갈 수 있어요
nagago sipeoyo	nagal su isseoyo

Don't (Imperative) / Whether or not

Don't (Imperative)	Whether or not		
나가지 마세요	나가는지	나갔는지	나갈지
nagaji maseyo	naganeunji	naganneunji	nagaljji

(tell someone) that / (tell someone) to

(tell someone) that	(tell someone) to
나간다고	나가라고
nagandago	nagarago

Sample Sentences

1. 저도 이제 나갈 거예요.
   I'm going to leave now, too.

2. 여기서 나가고 싶어요.
   I want to get out of here.

3. 정수 씨가 언제 나갔는지 알아요?
   Do you know when Jeong-su left?

4. 방금 나간 사람 누구예요?
   Who is the person who just left?

5. 윤지 씨가 벌써 나갔는지 몰랐어요.
   I didn't know Yoonji already left.

Quiz

1. 빨리 (   ).
   I want to get out of here quickly.

2. 아까 (   ) 사람 누군지 알아요?
   Do you know the person who left earlier?

3. 진수 씨가 언제 (   ) 알아요?
   Do you know when Jinsoo left?

울다

to cry, to sob

Conjugation

Present	Past	Future / Guessing	Present Progressive
울어요	울었어요	울 거예요	울고 있어요
ureoyo	ureosseoyo	ul geoyeyo	ulgo isseoyo

Imperative

우세요	울어요	울어	울어라
useyo	ureoyo	ureo	ureora

Modifier

운	우는	울	울던	울었던
un	uneun	ul	uldeon	ureottteon

Want

울고 싶어요
ulgo sipeoyo

Can

울 수 있어요
ul su isseoyo

Don't (Imperative)

울지 마세요
ulji maseyo

Whether or not

우는지	울었는지	울지
uneunji	ureonneunji	uljji

(tell someone) that

운다고
undago

(tell someone) to

울라고
ullago

Sample Sentences

1. 밤마다 옆집 아기가 울어요.
   The baby next door cries every night.

2. 슬프면 참지 말고 그냥 울어.
   If you are sad, don't hold back and just cry.

3. 그 영화 보고 안 울었어요?
   You didn't cry after watching that movie?

4. 제가 어떤 말을 해도 울지 마세요.
   Please don't cry no matter what I say.

5. 일이 잘 안 돼서 울고 싶어요.
   Things didn't go well, so I want to cry.

Quiz

1. 지민 씨는 그 책을 읽고 안 (   ).
   Jimin didn't cry after she read the book.

2. 무슨 일이 있어도 (   ).
   No matter what happens, please don't cry.

3. 엄마한테 혼나서 (   ).
   I was scolded by my mom, so I want to cry.

Answers :
1. 울었어요 / 2. 울지 마세요 / 3. 울고 싶어요

누르다

to press;
to hit (a button)

Conjugation

Present	Past	Future / Guessing	Present Progressive
눌러요	눌렀어요	누를 거예요	누르고 있어요
nulleoyo	nulleosseoyo	nureul geoyeyo	nureugo isseoyo

Imperative

누르세요	눌러요	눌러	눌러라
nureuseyo	nulleoyo	nulleo	nulleora

Modifier

누른	누르는	누를	누르던	눌렀던
nureun	nureuneun	nureul	nureudeon	nulleottteon

Want / Can

Want	Can
누르고 싶어요	누를 수 있어요
nureugo sipeoyo	nureul su isseoyo

Don't (Imperative) / Whether or not

Don't (Imperative)	Whether or not		
누르지 마세요	누르는지	눌렀는지	누를지
nureuji maseyo	nureuneunji	nulleonneunji	nureuljji

(tell someone) that / (tell someone) to

(tell someone) that	(tell someone) to
누른다고	누르라고
nureundago	nureurago

Sample Sentences

1. 더 세게 눌러요.
   Please push it hard.

2. 언니가 이럴 때는 F5키를 누르라고 했어요.
   My older sister told me to press the F5 button when that happens.

3. 아프니까 너무 세게 누르지 마세요.
   It hurts, so please don't press on it too hard.

4. 이 단추 누가 눌렀는지 알아요?
   Do you know who pushed this button?

5. 주문을 하실 때는 이 버튼을 누르세요.
   When you order, please push this button.

Quiz

1. 엄마가 밥을 하려면 이 버튼을 (   ) 하셨어요.
   My mom told me to press this button to cook the rice.

2. 엔터키 누가 (   ) 말해 주세요.
   Please tell me who pressed(hit) the enter button.

3. 필요한 게 있으면 이 버튼을 (   ).
   If you need anything, please push this button.

Answers :
1. 누르라고 / 2. 눌렀는지 / 3. 누르세요 or 눌러요.

129

밀다
to push

The Korean Verbs Guide - vol.2

Conjugation

Present	Past	Future / Guessing	Present Progressive
밀어요	밀었어요	밀 거예요	밀고 있어요
mireoyo	mireosseoyo	mil geoyeyo	milgo isseoyo

Imperative

미세요	밀어요	밀어	밀어라
miseyo	mireoyo	mireo	mireora

Modifier

민	미는	밀	밀던	밀었던
min	mineun	mil	mildeon	mireottteon

Want

밀고 싶어요
milgo sipeoyo

Can

밀 수 있어요
mil su isseoyo

Don't (Imperative)

밀지 마세요	미는지
milji maseyo	mineunji

Whether or not

밀었는지	밀지
mireonneunji	miljji

(tell someone) that

민다고
mindago

(tell someone) to

밀라고
millago

131

Sample Sentences

1. 제 등을 누가 밀었는지 아세요?
   Do you know who pushed me in the back?

2. 누가 뒤에서 자꾸 밀어요.
   Someone keeps pushing me in the back.

3. 위험하니까 여기서 밀지 마세요.
   Don't push me here because it's dangerous.

4. 두 손으로 동시에 미세요.
   Please push it with both hands at the same time.

5. 제가 뒤에서 밀었어요.
   I pushed it from behind.

Quiz

1. 버스 정류장에서 누가 절 (   ) 아세요?
   Do you know who pushed me at the bus stop?

2. 승민 씨가 자꾸 (   ).
   Seung-min keeps pushing me.

3. 제가 신호를 보내면 (   ).
   Push it when I give you the sign.

Answers :
1. 밀었는지 / 2. 밀어요 / 3. 미세요 or 밀어요

The Korean Verbs Guide - vol.2

당기다
to pull

Conjugation

당기다
dang-gi-da

Present	Past	Future / Guessing	Present Progressive
당겨요	당겼어요	당길 거예요	당기고 있어요
dang-gyeoyo	dang-gyeosseoyo	dang-gil geoyeyo	dang-gigo isseoyo

Imperative

당기세요	당겨요	당겨	당겨라
dang-giseyo	dang-gyeoyo	dang-gyeo	dang-gyeora

Modifier

당긴	당기는	당길	당기던	당겼던
dang-gin	dang-gineun	dang-gil	dang-gideon	dang-gyeottteon

Want	Can
당기고 싶어요	당길 수 있어요
dang-gigo sipeoyo	dang-gil su isseoyo

Don't (Imperative)	Whether or not		
당기지 마세요	당기는지	당겼는지	당길지
dang-giji maseyo	dang-gineunji	dang-gyeonneunji	dang-giljji

(tell someone) that	(tell someone) to
당긴다고	당기라고
dang-gindago	dang-girago

Sample Sentences

1. 여기에는 이 줄을 당기라고 써 있어요.
   Here, it says to pull this cord.

2. 그쪽에서 당기세요.
   Please pull it from there.

3. 어디를 당기는지 아세요?
   Do you know where we should pull?

4. 밀지 말고 당기세요.
   Please don't push, but pull.

5. 더 세게 당길 수 있어요?
   Can you pull it harder?

Quiz

1. 줄을 (   ) 써 있어요?
   Does it say to pull the cord?

2. 지영 씨가 (   )요.
   Jiyoung, you pull it, please.

3. 혼자 (   )?
   Can you pull it by yourself?

그냥 아무 곳에나
놓으세요.

Just put it anywhere please.

놓다

to put, to place (something)

Conjugation

Present	Past	Future / Guessing	Present Progressive
놓아요	놓았어요	놓을 거예요	놓고 있어요
noayo	noasseoyo	no-eul geoyeyo	noko isseoyo

Imperative

놓으세요	놓아요	놓아	놓아라
no-euseyo	noayo	noa	noara

Modifier

놓은	놓는	놓을	놓던	놓았던
no-eun	nonneun	noeul	noteon	noattteon

Want	Can
놓고 싶어요	놓을 수 있어요
noko sipeoyo	no-eul su isseoyo

Don't (Imperative)	Whether or not		
놓지 마세요	놓는지	놓았는지	놓을지
nochi maseyo	nonneunji	noanneunji	no-euljji

(tell someone) that	(tell someone) to
놓는다고	놓으라고
nonneundago	no-eurago

The Korean Verbs Guide - vol.2

Sample Sentences

1. 이 꽃병은 식탁 위에 놓고 싶어요.
   I want to put this flower vase on the dining table.

2. 화분을 어디에 놓을지 아직도 못 정했어요?
   Have you still not decided where you are going to put the flowerpot?

3. 그냥 아무 곳에나 놓으세요.
   Just put it anywhere, please.

4. 제가 가방을 여기에 놓을지 어떻게 알았어요?
   How did you know I would put my bag here?

5. 새로 산 침대는 어디에 놓을 거예요?
   Where are you going to put the new bed that you bought?

Quiz

1. 새로 산 의자는 책상 앞에 (   ).
   I want to put the new chair I bought in front of the desk.

2. 이 토끼 인형 어디에 (   ) 정했어요?
   Have you decided where to put this stuffed rabbit?

3. 제 옆에 (   ).
   Please put it next to me.

끝나다

to be over;
something is finished

Conjugation

Present	Past	Future / Guessing	Present Progressive
끝나요	끝났어요	끝날 거예요	—
kkeunnayo	kkeunnasseoyo	kkeunnal geoyeyo	

Imperative

—	—	—	—

Modifier

끝난	끝나는	끝날	끝나던	끝났던
kkeunnan	kkeunnaneun	kkeunnal	kkeunadeon	kkeunnattteon

Want	Can
—	끝날 수 있어요
	kkeunnal su isseoyo

Don't (Imperative)	Whether or not		
—	끝나는지	끝났는지	끝날지
	kkeunnaneunji	kkeunnanneunji	kkeunnaljji

(tell someone) that	(tell someone) to
끝난다고	—
kkeunnandago	

Sample Sentences

1. 언제 끝났어요?
   When did it finish?

2. 내일이면 끝난다고 했어요.
   They said it will be finished tomorrow.

3. 곧 방학이 끝날 거예요.
   The school vacation will be over soon.

4. 행사가 벌써 끝났는지 몰랐어요.
   I didn't know the event was already over.

5. 이 영화 몇 시에 끝나는지 아세요?
   Do you know what time the movie finishes?

Quiz

1. 다음 주에 (   ) 들었어요.
   I heard it will be finished next week.

2. 한 시간 후에 수업이 (   ).
   The class will be over in an hour.

3. 학교가 몇 시에 (   ) 물어보세요.
   Please ask her what time school finishes.

가르치다
to teach

Conjugation

가르치다
ga-reu-chi-da

Present	Past	Future / Guessing	Present Progressive
가르쳐요	가르쳤어요	가르칠 거예요	가르치고 있어요
gareuchyeoyo	gareuchyeosseoyo	gareuchil geoyeyo	gareuchigo isseoyo

Imperative

가르치세요	가르쳐요	가르쳐	가르쳐라
gareuchiseyo	gareuchyeoyo	gareuchyeo	gareuchyeora

Modifier

가르친	가르치는	가르칠	가르치던	가르쳤던
gareuchin	gareuchineun	gareuchil	gareuchideon	gareuchyeottteon

Want	Can
가르치고 싶어요	가르칠 수 있어요
gareuchigo sipeoyo	gareuchil su isseoyo

Don't (Imperative)	Whether or not		
가르치지 마세요	가르치는지	가르쳤는지	가르칠지
gareuchiji maseyo	gareuchineunji	gareuchyeonneunji	gareuchiljji

(tell someone) that	(tell someone) to
가르친다고	가르치라고
gareuchindago	gareuchirago

Sample Sentences

1. 그런 건 아이들한테 가르치지 마세요.
   Please don't teach such things to the children.

2. 저는 고등학교에서 음악을 가르쳐요.
   I teach music at a high school.

3. 어디에서 가르친다고 했죠?
   Where did you say you teach at?

4. 이 반은 제니퍼 선생님이 영어를 가르칠 거예요.
   Teacher Jennifer will teach English in this class.

5. 어제 가르친 중국어 단어를 학생들이 벌써 다 잊어버렸어요.
   The students already forgot all the Chinese words I taught them yesterday.

Quiz

1. 희수 씨는 대학교에서 수학을 (   ).
   Heesu teaches math at a university.

2. 뭐 (   ) 했죠?
   What did you say you teach?

3. 지난 주에 (   ) 수학 공식을 기억하는 학생이 한 명도
   없어요.
   There's no student who remembers the math formula I taught last
   week.

Answers :
1. 가르쳐요 / 2. 가르친다고 / 3. 가르친

내다

to hand in, to submit; to pay;
to publish; to suggest (idea);
to put up (an advertisement)

Conjugation

Present	Past	Future / Guessing	Present Progressive
내요	냈어요	낼 거예요	내고 있어요
naeyo	naesseoyo	nael geoyeyo	naego isseoyo

Imperative

내세요	내요	내	내라
naeseyo	naeyo	nae	naera

Modifier

낸	내는	낼	내던	냈던
naen	naeneun	nael	naedeon	naettteon

Want	Can
내고 싶어요	낼 수 있어요
naego sipeoyo	nael su isseoyo

Don't (Imperative)	Whether or not		
내지 마세요	내는지	냈는지	낼지
naeji maseyo	naeneunji	naenneunji	naeljji

(tell someone) that	(tell someone) to
낸다고	내라고
naendago	naerago

Sample Sentences

1. 누가 돈 낼지 정했어요?
   Have you guys decided who's going to pay?

2. 제가 냈어요.
   I paid.

3. 신문에 광고를 어떻게 내는지 아세요?
   Do you know how to put up an ad in a newspaper?

4. 어제 회사에 사표를 냈어요.
   I submitted my resignation letter at work yesterday.

5. 핸드폰으로 세금 낼 수 있어요?
   Can we pay the tax with our cellphone?

Quiz

1. 지석 씨가 (   ).
   Jiseok paid.

2. 이번 커피 값은 누가 (   ) 정했어요?
   Have you guys decided who's going to pay for the coffee this time?

3. 인터넷으로 벌금 (   )?
   Can we pay the fine over the internet?

Answers :
1. 냈어요 / 2. 낼지 / 3. 낼 수 있어요

The Korean Verbs Guide - vol.2

빼다

to take out, to
pull out

Conjugation

빼다
ppae-da

Present	Past	Future / Guessing	Present Progressive
빼요	뺐어요	뺄 거예요	빼고 있어요
ppaeyo	ppaesseoyo	ppael geoyeyo	ppaego isseoyo

Imperative

빼세요	빼요	빼	빼라
ppaeseyo	ppaeyo	ppae	ppaera

Modifier

뺀	빼는	뺄	빼던	뺐던
ppaen	ppaeneun	ppael	ppaedeon	ppaettteon

Want

빼고 싶어요
ppaego sipeoyo

Can

뺄 수 있어요
ppael su isseoyo

Don't (Imperative)

빼지 마세요
ppaeji maseyo

Whether or not

빼는지	뺐는지	뺄지
ppaeneunji	ppaenneunji	ppaeljji

(tell someone) that

뺀다고
ppaendago

(tell someone) to

빼라고
ppaerago

Sample Sentences

1. 주머니에서 손 빼세요.
   Please take your hands out of your pocket.

2. 왜 저를 팀에서 뺐어요?
   Why did you take me off of the team?

3. 못이 위험하니까 빼라고 말했는데 아직 그대로 있네요.
   I told them to pull this nail out because it is dangerous, but it is still here.

4. 저는 작년에 사랑니를 뺐어요.
   I got my wisdom teeth pulled last year.

5. 오늘 세미나에 안 온 사람들 이름을 명단에서 빼고 있어요.
   I'm taking off the names of the people who didn't come to the seminar today.

Quiz

1. 저를 그룹에서 (   ) 이유가 뭔가요?
   What is the reason that you took me out of the group?

2. 못을 (   ) 했는데 왜 안 (   )?
   I told you to pull this nail out, but why didn't you do it?

3. 어제 드디어 치과에서 사랑니 (   ).
   I finally got my wisdom teeth taken out yesterday at the dentist.

넣다

to put in, to insert

Conjugation

Present	Past	Future / Guessing	Present Progressive
넣어요	넣었어요	넣을 거예요	넣고 있어요
neo-eoyo	neo-eosseoyo	neo-eul geoyeyo	neoko isseoyo

Imperative

넣으세요	넣어요	넣어	넣어라
neo-euseyo	neo-eoyo	neo-eo	neo-eora

Modifier

넣은	넣는	넣을	넣던	넣었던
neo-eun	neonneun	neo-eul	neoteon	neo-eottteon

Want	Can
넣고 싶어요	넣을 수 있어요
neoko sipeoyo	neo-eul su isseoyo

Don't (Imperative)	Whether or not		
넣지 마세요	넣는지	넣었는지	넣을지
neochi maseyo	neonneunji	neo-eonneunji	neo-euljji

(tell someone) that	(tell someone) to
넣는다고	넣으라고
neonneundago	neo-eurago

Sample Sentences

1. 제 커피에는 설탕 넣지 마세요.
   Please do not put sugar in my coffee.

2. 제 가방에 뭐 넣었어요?
   What did you put in my bag?

3. 책은 가방에 넣으세요.
   Please put the book in the bag.

4. 여기에 100원짜리 동전만 넣으라고 써 있어요.
   It says to only put 100 won coins in here.

5. 아까 케이크에 넣은 우유가 상했었나 봐요.
   The milk that we put in the cake a little while ago seems to have been spoiled.

Quiz

1. 제 수프에 후추 (   ).
   Please don't put pepper in my soup.

2. 돈은 주머니에 (   ).
   Please put the money in your pocket.

3. 샌드위치에 (   ) 치즈가 맛있어요.
   The cheese we put in the sandwich is yummy

Answers :
1. 넣지 마세요 / 2. 넣으세요 or 넣어요 / 3. 넣은

The Korean Verbs Guide - vol.2

요즘 재미있는 걸 배우고 있어요.

I'm learning something interesting these days.

배우다

to learn

Conjugation

배우다
bae-u-da

Present	Past	Future / Guessing	Present Progressive
배워요	배웠어요	배울 거예요	배우고 있어요
baewoyo	baewosseoyo	baeul geoyeyo	baeugo isseoyo

Imperative

배우세요	배워요	배워	배워라
baeuseyo	baewoyo	baewo	baewora

Modifier

배운	배우는	배울	배우던	배웠던
bae-un	bae-uneun	bae-ul	bae-udeon	baewottteon

Want

배우고 싶어요
bae-ugo sipeoyo

Can

배울 수 있어요
bae-ul su isseoyo

Don't (Imperative)

배우지 마세요
bae-uji maseyo

Whether or not

배우는지	배웠는지	배울지
bae-uneunji	baewonneunji	bae-uljji

(tell someone) that

배운다고
bae-undago

(tell someone) to

배우라고
bae-urago

Sample Sentences

1. 우리 같이 요리 배워요.
   Let's learn how to cook together.

2. 저 사람한테는 배우지 마세요.
   Don't learn from that person.

3. 어디서 한국어 배울 수 있어요?
   Where can I learn Korean?

4. 올 여름에는 서핑을 배울 거예요.
   I'm going to learn how to surf this summer.

5. 지난주에 뭐 배웠는지 기억나요?
   Do you remember what we learned last week?

Quiz

1. 이번 여름에 같이 수영 (   ).
   Let's learn how to swim together this summer.

2. 내년 봄부터는 피아노 (   ).
   Starting from next spring, I'm going to learn how to play the piano.

3. 지난 금요일에 뭐 (   ) 말해 주세요.
   Please tell me what you learned last Friday.

The Korean Verbs Guide - vol.2

되다

to become;
(something) is done

Conjugation

	Present	Past	Future / Guessing	Present Progressive
	돼요	됐어요	될 거예요	되고 있어요
	dwaeyo	dwaesseoyo	doel geoyeyo	doego isseoyo

Imperative

되세요	돼요	돼	돼라
doeseyo	dwaeyo	dwae	dwaera

Modifier

된	되는	될	되던	됐던
doen	doeneun	doel	doedeon	dwaettteon

Want

되고 싶어요
doego sipeoyo

Can

될 수 있어요
doel su isseoyo

Don't (Imperative)

되지 마세요
doeji maseyo

Whether or not

되는지	됐는지	될지
doeneunji	dwaenneunji	doeljji

(tell someone) that

된다고
doendago

(tell someone) to

되라고
doerago

Sample Sentences

1. 벌써 겨울이 됐어요.
   It has already become winter.

2. 피아니스트가 되는 것이 꿈이었어요.
   My dream was to become a pianist.

3. 누가 1등이 됐는지 너무 궁금해요.
   I curious to know who became number 1.

4. 조금만 기다리면 요리가 다 된다고 했어요.
   He said if you wait just a little, the food would be done.

5. 오늘 너무 더워서 얼음이 물이 됐어요.
   Today was so hot that the ice became water.

Quiz

1. 대회 연습을 하는 사이에 벌써 1월이 (   ).
   While we were practicing for the contest, it had already became January.

2. 저는 어렸을 때 비행기 조종사가 (   ) 것이 꿈이었어요.
   When I was little, my dream was to become a pilot.

3. 누가 대통령이 (   ) 알아요?
   Do you know who became the president?

Answers :
1. 됐어요 / 2. 되는 / 3. 됐는지

161

걸다
to hang

Conjugation

걸다
geol-da

Present	Past	Future / Guessing	Present Progressive
걸어요	걸었어요	걸 거예요	걸고 있어요
georeoyo	georeosseoyo	geol geoyeyo	geolgo isseoyo
			걸려 있어요*
			geollyeo isseoyo

Imperative

거세요	걸어요	걸어	걸어라
geoseyo	georeoyo	georeo	georeora

Modifier

건	거는	걸	걸던	걸었던
geon	geoneun	geol	geoldeon	georeottteon

Want

걸고 싶어요
geolgo sipeoyo

Can

걸 수 있어요
geol su isseoyo

Don't (Imperative)

걸지 마세요
geolji maseyo

Whether or not

거는지	걸었는지	걸지
geoneunji	georeonneunji	geoljji

(tell someone) that

건다고
geondago

(tell someone) to

걸라고
geollago

*present status

Sample Sentences

1. 이 시계 어디에 걸 거예요?
   Where are you going to hang up this clock?

2. 건물 왼쪽에 간판을 걸라고 시켰어요.
   I ordered them to hang up a sign on the left side of the building.

3. 이 벽에는 아무것도 걸지 마세요.
   Don't hang up anything on this wall.

4. 옷걸이에 걸었던 옷이 조금 구겨졌어요.
   The clothes that I hung up on the hanger became wrinkled.

5. 망치하고 못만 있으면 이런 작은 시계는 벽에 금방 걸 수 있어요.
   If you have a hammer and a nail, you can hang up a small clock, like this one, quickly.

Quiz

1. 이 사진 도대체 언제 벽에 (   )?
   When on earth are you going to hang up this picture?

2. 엄마가 이걸 이쪽 벽에 (   ) 하셨어요.
   My mom told me to hang this up on the wall over here.

3. 저 옷걸이에는 아무 옷도 (   ).
   Don't hang up any clothes on that hanger.

Answers :
1. 걸 거예요 / 2. 걸라고 / 3. 걸지 마세요

The Korean Verbs Guide - vol.2

예쁘다
to be pretty,
to be beautiful

Conjugation

Present	Past	Future / Guessing	Present Progressive
예뻐요	예뻤어요	예쁠 거예요	—
yeppeoyo	yeppeosseoyo	yeppeul geoyeyo	

Imperative			
—	—	—	—

Modifier				
예쁜	—	예쁠	예쁘던	예뻤던
yeppeun		yeppeul	yeppeudeon	yeppeottteon

Want	Can
—	예쁠 수 있어요
	yeppeul su isseoyo

Don't (Imperative)	Whether or not		
—	예쁜지	예뻤는지	예쁠지
	yeppeunji	yeppeonneunji	yeppeuljji

(tell someone) that	(tell someone) to
예쁘다고	—
yeppeudago	

Sample Sentences

1. 반에서 제일 예뻤던 아이라고 기억해요.
   I remember her being the prettiest girl in our class.

2. 어떤 색이 예쁠지 모르겠어요.
   I don't know what color would look pretty.

3. 이 글씨체 너무 예뻐요.
   This writing style is so pretty.

4. 선물을 예쁜 포장지에 싸서 주고 싶어요.
   I want to wrap the present in pretty wrapping paper, then give it to her.

5. 이 가방 친구들이 예쁘다고 칭찬했어요.
   My friends complimented my bag, saying that it was pretty.

Quiz

1. 수현 씨가 쓰고 있는 모자 정말 (   ).
   The hat Soohyeon is wearing is really pretty.

2. 편지는 (   ) 봉투에 담으세요.
   Please put your letter in a pretty envelope.

3. 같은 반 친구가 제가 어제 새로 산 치마가 (   ) 했어요.
   My classmate told me that the skirt I bought yesterday is pretty.

You can download the audio recordings for the words and sample sentences used in this book for free at TalkToMeInKorean.com/audio.